WALTZES & POLKAS
FOR EASY CLASSICAL PIANO
ARRANGED BY PHILLIP KEVEREN

— PIANO LEVEL —
INTERMEDIATE

ISBN 978-1-4950-6397-8

7777 W. BLUEMOUND RD. P.O. BOX 13819 MILWAUKEE, WI 53213

Visit Hal Leonard Online at
www.halleonard.com

Visit Phillip at
www.phillipkeveren.com

PREFACE

Dance and music go together like salt and pepper or peanut butter and jelly – some, including me, would say chocolate and coffee! Of all the dances to develop through the ages, the waltz and the polka seem to be among the most popular. This collection gives a nod to both "serious" composers and "popular" songwriters who have written music in these genres.

Whether relatively new (Billy Joel's "Piano Man" from the 1970s) or relatively old (Johann Strauss Jr.'s "By the Beautiful Blue Danube" from the 1860s), all of these pieces make compelling piano solos worthy of study. And fun, by the way!

Sincerely,

Phillip Keveren

BIOGRAPHY

Phillip Keveren, a multi-talented keyboard artist and composer, has composed original works in a variety of genres from piano solo to symphonic orchestra. Mr. Keveren gives frequent concerts and workshops for teachers and their students in the United States, Canada, Europe, and Asia. Mr. Keveren holds a B.M. in composition from California State University Northridge and a M.M. in composition from the University of Southern California.

CONTENTS

ACCELERATION WALTZ

By JOHANN STRAUSS JR.
Arranged by Phillip Keveren

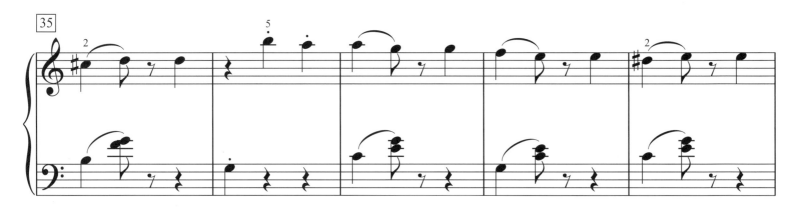

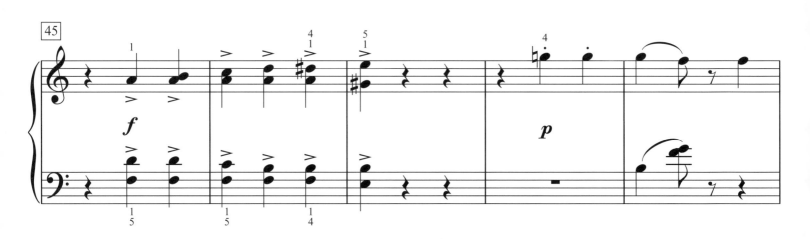

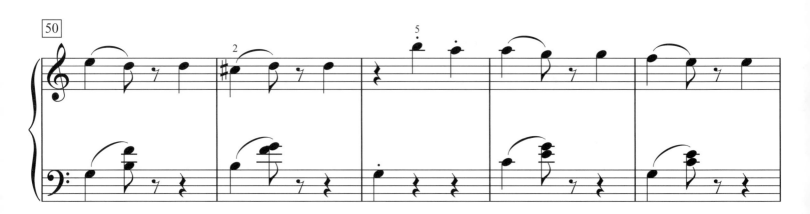

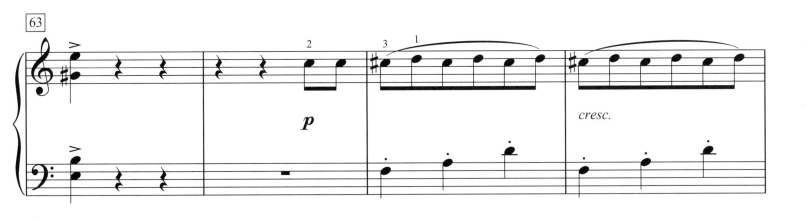

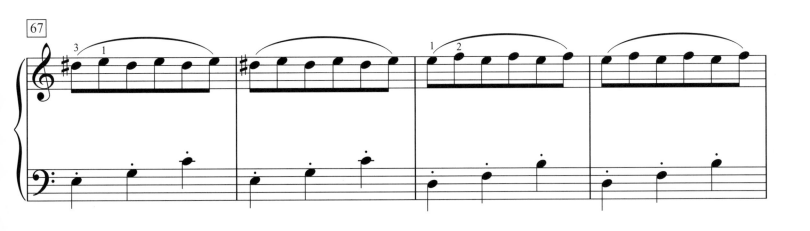

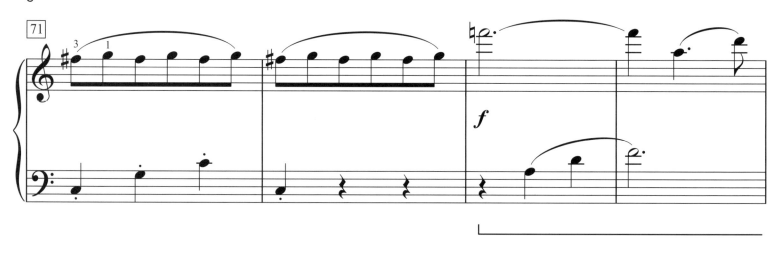

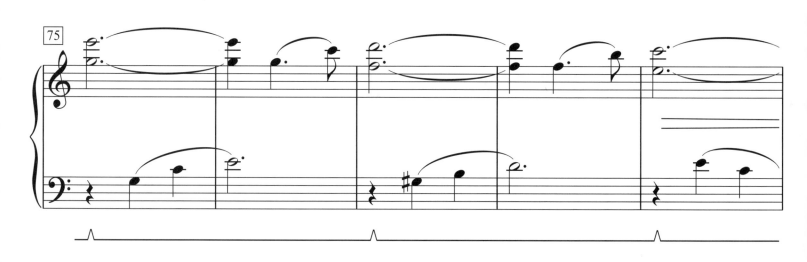

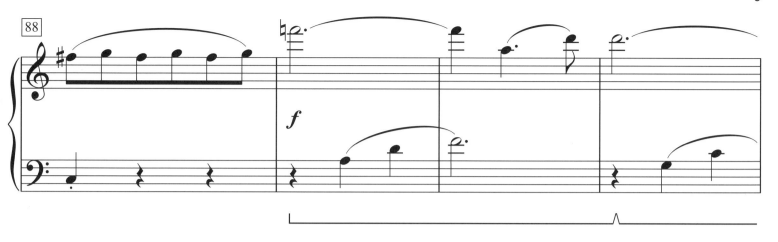

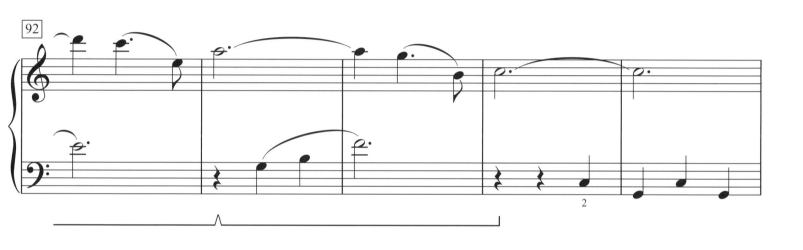

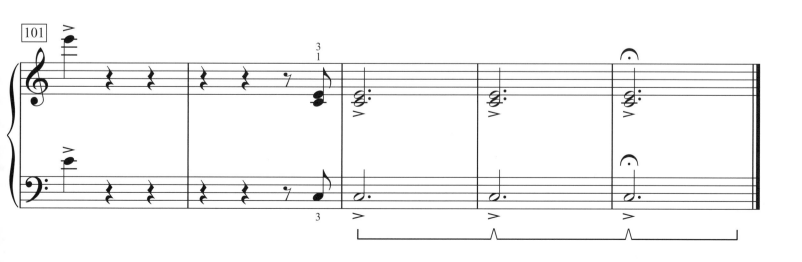

BEER BARREL POLKA
(Roll Out the Barrel)

Based on the European success "Skoda Lasky"*
By LEW BROWN, WLADIMIR A. TIMM,
JAROMIR VEJVODA and VASEK ZEMAN
Arranged by Phillip Keveren

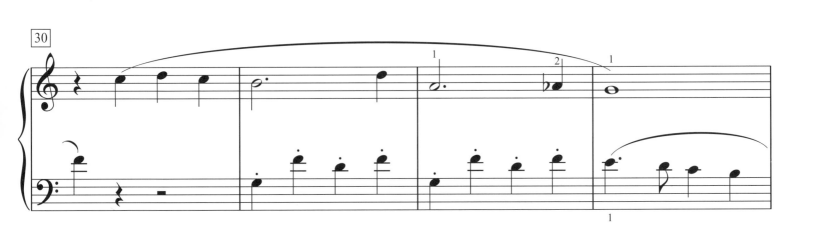

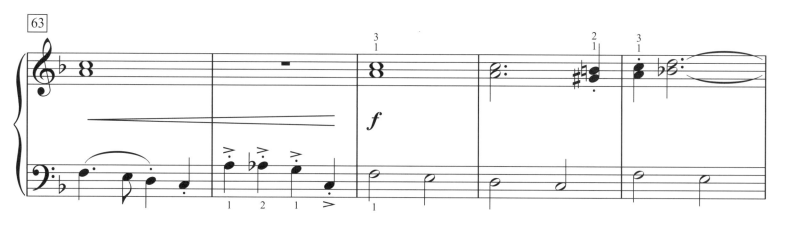

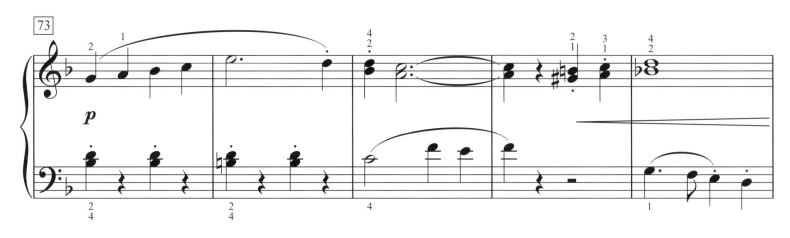

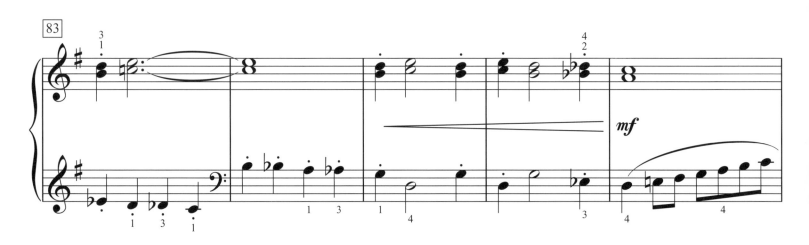

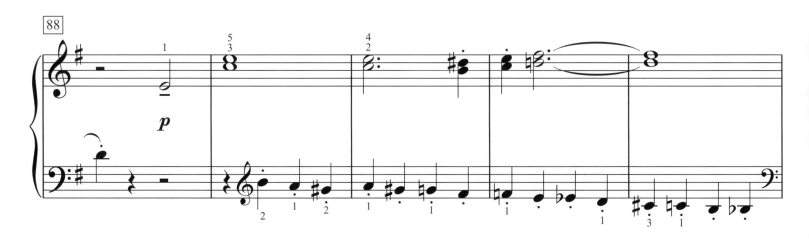

BITTE SCHÖN!
(If You Please Polka)

By JOHANN STRAUSS JR.
Arranged by Phillip Keveren

Jauntily (♩ = 96)

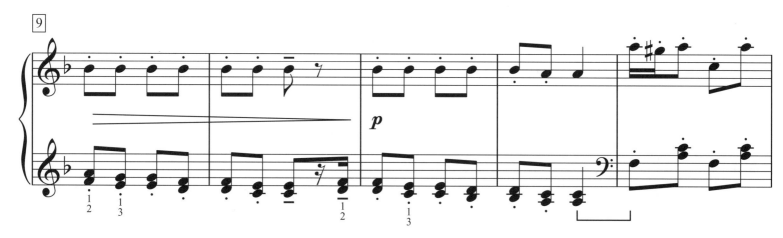

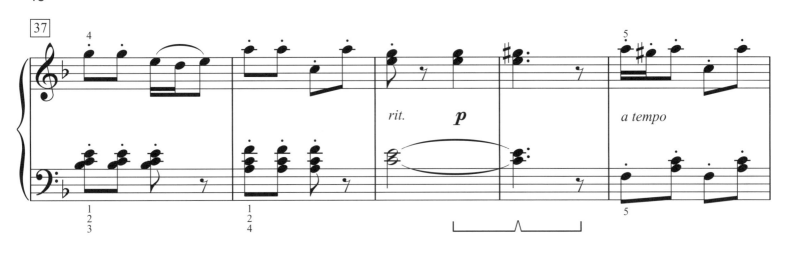

BY THE BEAUTIFUL DANUBE

By JOHANN STRAUSS JR.
Arranged by Phillip Keveren

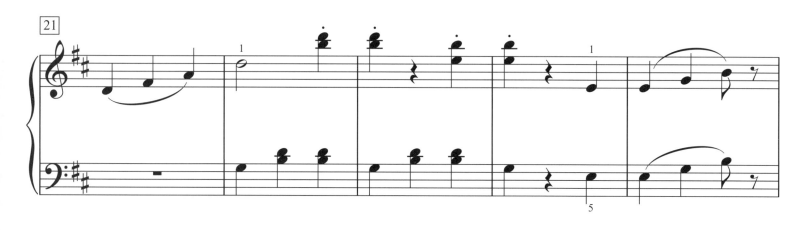

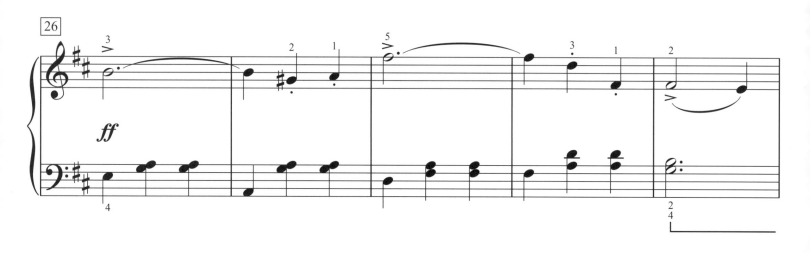

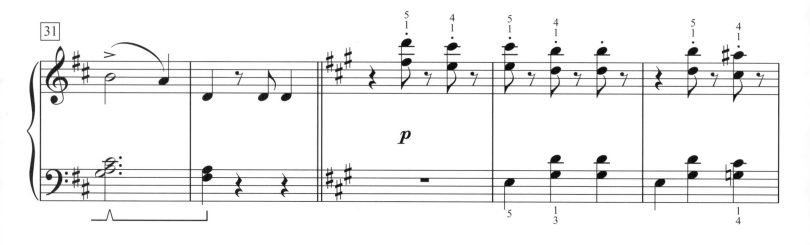

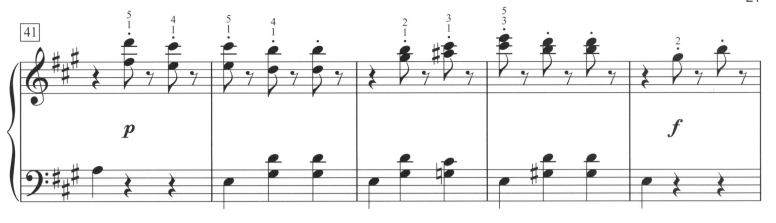

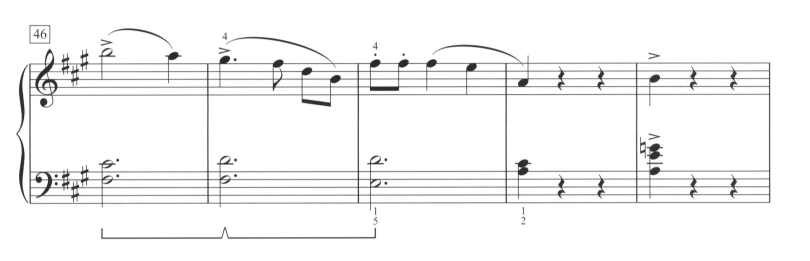

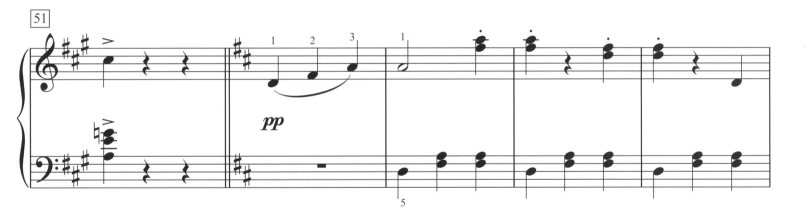

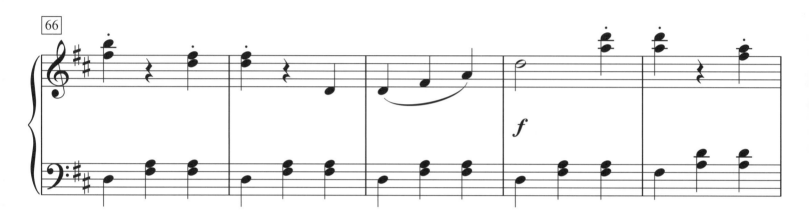

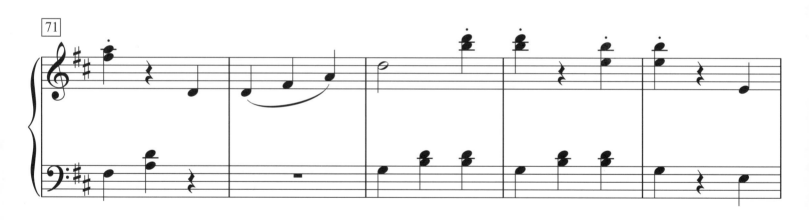

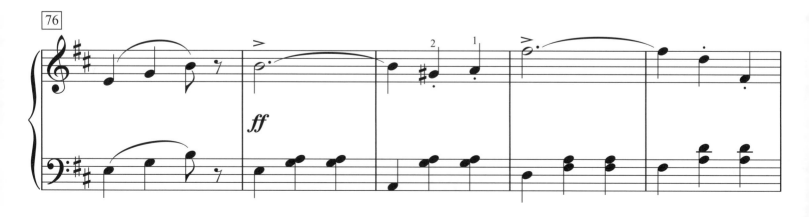

CLARINET POLKA

TRADITIONAL
Arranged by Phillip Keveren

FASCINATION
(Valse Tzigane)

By F.D. MARCHETTI
Arranged by Phillip Keveren

THE GODFATHER WALTZ

from the Paramount Pictures THE GODFATHER, GODFATHER II, and GODFATHER III

By NINO ROTA
Arranged by Phillip Keveren

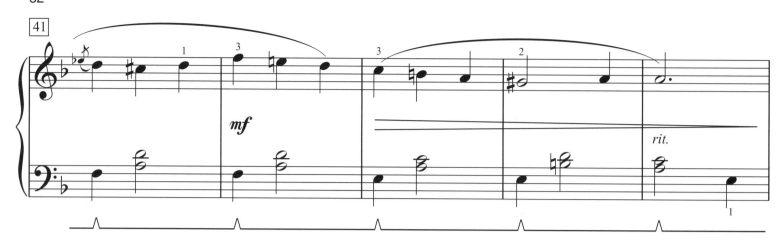

LIECHTENSTEINER POLKA

Words and Music by EDMUND KOETSCHER
and RUDI LINDT
Arranged by Phillip Keveren

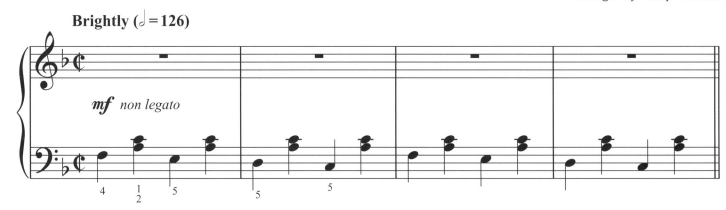

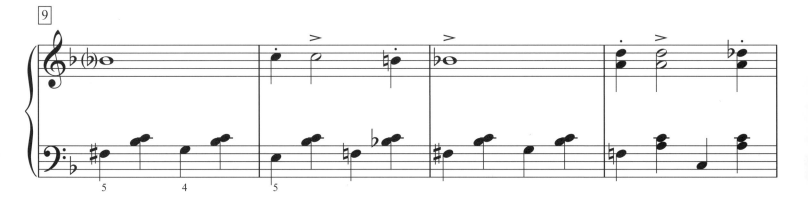

PENNSYLVANIA POLKA

Words and Music by LESTER LEE
and ZEKE MANNERS
Arranged by Phillip Keveren

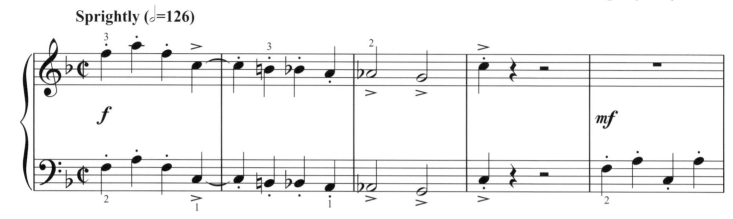

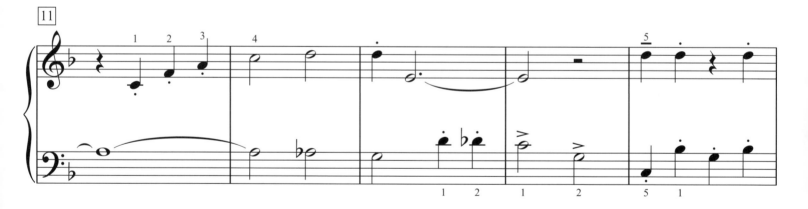

PIANO MAN

Words and Music by
BILLY JOEL
Arranged by Phillip Keveren

Flowing (♩ = 176)

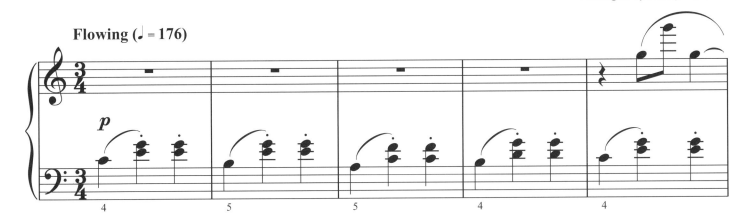

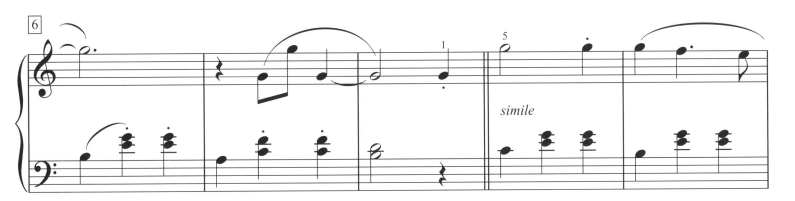

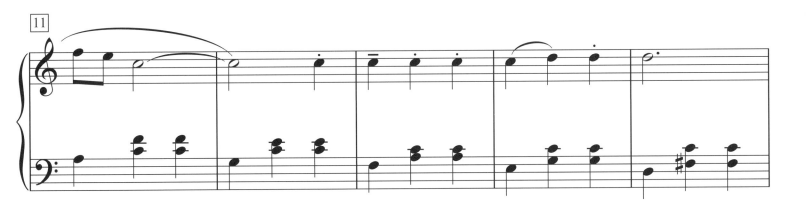

PIZZICATO POLKA

By JOHANN STRAUSS JR.
Arranged by Phillip Keveren

Allegro (♩ = 80)

sempre staccato

QUE SERA, SERA

(Whatever Will Be, Will Be)
from THE MAN WHO KNEW TOO MUCH

Words and Music by JAY LIVINGSTON
and RAYMOND B. EVANS
Arranged by Phillip Keveren

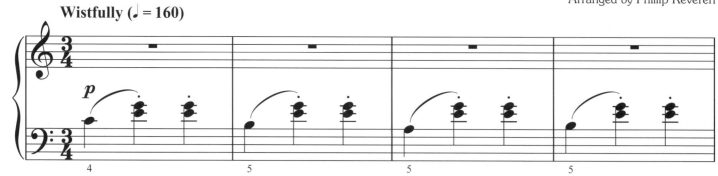

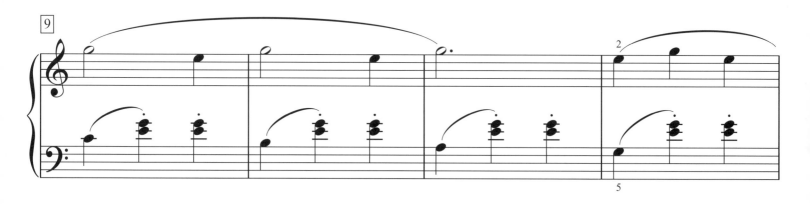

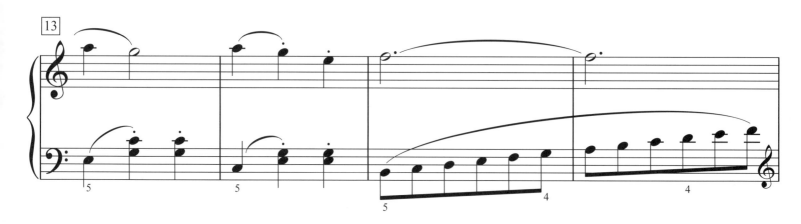

THE SLEEPING BEAUTY WALTZ

By PYOTR IL'YICH TCHAIKOVSKY
Arranged by Phillip Keveren

TENNESSEE WALTZ

Words and Music by REDD STEWART
and PEE WEE KING
Arranged by Phillip Keveren

WALTZ OF THE FLOWERS

from THE NUTCRACKER

By PYOTR IL'YICH TCHAIKOVSKY
Arranged by Phillip Keveren

THE PHILLIP KEVEREN SERIES

PIANO SOLO —
Late Intermediate/Early Advanced Level

ABOVE ALL
00311024..$11.95

AMERICANA
00311348..$10.95

THE BEATLES
00306412..$14.99

THE BEATLES FOR CLASSICAL PIANO
00312189..$14.99

BEST PIANO SOLOS
00312546..$12.99

BLESSINGS
00156601..$12.99

BROADWAY'S BEST
00310669..$12.95

CANZONE ITALIANA
00312106..$12.99

A CELTIC CHRISTMAS
00310629..$12.99

THE CELTIC COLLECTION
00310549..$12.95

CHRISTMAS MEDLEYS
00311414..$12.99

CHRISTMAS AT THE MOVIES
00312190..$12.99

CHRISTMAS WORSHIP MEDLEYS
00311769..$12.99

CINEMA CLASSICS
00310607..$12.95

CLASSIC WEDDING SONGS
00311101..$10.95

CLASSICAL FOLK
00311292..$10.95

CLASSICAL JAZZ
00311083..$12.95

COLDPLAY FOR CLASSICAL PIANO
00137779..$14.99

CONTEMPORARY WEDDING SONGS
00311103..$12.99

DISNEY SONGS FOR CLASSICAL PIANO
00311754..$14.99

FAVORITE WEDDING SONGS
00311881..$12.99

FIDDLIN' AT THE PIANO
00315974..$12.99

THE FILM SCORE COLLECTION
00311811..$12.99

GOSPEL GREATS
00144351..$12.99

THE GREAT MELODIES
00312084..$12.99

GREAT STANDARDS
00311157..$12.95

THE HYMN COLLECTION
00311071..$11.95

HYMN MEDLEYS
00311349..$10.95

HYMNS WITH A TOUCH OF JAZZ
00311249..$10.95

I COULD SING OF YOUR LOVE FOREVER
00310905..$12.95

JINGLE JAZZ
00310762..$12.95

ELTON JOHN FOR CLASSICAL PIANO
00126449..$14.99

LET FREEDOM RING!
00310839..$9.95

ANDREW LLOYD WEBBER
00313227..$14.95

MANCINI MAGIC
00313523 ....$12.99

MORE DISNEY SONGS FOR CLASSICAL PIANO
00312113..$14.99

MOTOWN HITS
00311295..$12.95

PIAZZOLLA TANGOS
00306870..$12.95

RICHARD RODGERS CLASSICS
00310755..$12.95

SHOUT TO THE LORD!
00310699..$12.95

SMOOTH JAZZ
00311158..$12.95

THE SOUND OF MUSIC
00119403..$14.99

THE SPIRITUALS COLLECTION
00311978..$10.99

TREASURED HYMNS FOR CLASSICAL PIANO
00312112..$12.99

THE TWELVE KEYS OF CHRISTMAS
00144926..$12.99

WORSHIP WITH A TOUCH OF JAZZ
00294036..$12.99

YULETIDE JAZZ
00311911..$17.99

EASY PIANO —
Early Intermediate/Intermediate Level

AFRICAN-AMERICAN SPIRITUALS
00310610..$10.99

CELTIC DREAMS
00310973..$10.95

CHRISTMAS POPS
00311126..$14.99

CLASSIC POP/ROCK HITS
00311548..$12.95

A CLASSICAL CHRISTMAS
00310769..$10.95

CLASSICAL MOVIE THEMES
00310975..$10.99

CONTEMPORARY WORSHIP FAVORITES
00311805..$12.95

DISNEY SONGS FOR EASY CLASSICAL PIANO
00144352..$12.99

EARLY ROCK 'N' ROLL
00311093..$10.99

EASY WORSHIP MEDLEYS
00311997..$12.99

GEORGE GERSHWIN CLASSICS
00110374..$12.99

GOSPEL TREASURES
00310805..$11.95

THE VINCE GUARALDI COLLECTION
00306821..$12.95

IMMORTAL HYMNS
00310798..$10.95

JAZZ STANDARDS
00311294..$12.99

LOVE SONGS
00310744..$10.95

POP BALLADS
00220036..$12.95

POP GEMS OF THE '50s
00311406..$12.95

A RAGTIME CHRISTMAS
00102887 ....$10.99

RAGTIME CLASSICS
00311293..$10.95

SANTA SWINGS
00312028..$12.99

SONGS OF INSPIRATION
00103258..$12.99

SWEET LAND OF LIBERTY
00310840..$10.99

TIMELESS PRAISE
00310712..$12.95

10,000 REASONS
00126450..$14.99

TV THEMES
00311086..$10.95

21 GREAT CLASSICS
00310717..$12.99

WEEKLY WORSHIP
00145342..$16.99

BIG-NOTE PIANO —
Late Elementary/Early Intermediate Level

CHILDREN'S FAVORITE MOVIE SONGS
00310838..$10.95

CHRISTMAS MUSIC
00311247..$10.95

CONTEMPORARY HITS
00310907..$12.99

HOLIDAY FAVORITES
00311335..$12.95

HOW GREAT IS OUR GOD
00311402..$12.95

INTERNATIONAL FOLKSONGS
00311830..$12.99

JOY TO THE WORLD
00310888..$10.95

THE NUTCRACKER
00310908..$10.99

THIS IS YOUR TIME
00310956..$10.95

BEGINNING PIANO SOLOS —
Elementary/Late Elementary Level

AWESOME GOD
00311202..$10.95

CHRISTIAN CHILDREN'S FAVORITES
00310837..$10.95

CHRISTMAS FAVORITES
00311246..$10.95

CHRISTMAS TIME IS HERE
00311334..$12.99

CHRISTMAS TRADITIONS
00311117..$10.99

EASY HYMNS
00311250..$10.99

EVERLASTING GOD
00102710..$10.99

JAZZY TUNES
00311403..$10.95

KIDS' FAVORITES
00310822..$10.95

PIANO DUET

CLASSICAL THEME DUETS
00311350..$10.99

HYMN DUETS
00311544..$10.95

PRAISE & WORSHIP DUETS
00311203..$11.95

STAR WARS
00119405..$14.99

HAL•LEONARD® CORPORATION

7777 W. BLUEMOUND RD. P.O. BOX 13819 MILWAUKEE, WI 53213

www.halleonard.com

Prices, contents, and availability subject to change without notice.

0316